# The Correct Spelling
# & Exact Meaning

BOOKS BY RICHARD JONES

*Country of Air*

*At Last We Enter Paradise*

*A Perfect Time*

*48 Questions*

*The Blessing*

*Apropos of Nothing*

*The Correct Spelling & Exact Meaning*

# The Correct Spelling & Exact Meaning

RICHARD JONES

COPPER CANYON PRESS

PORT TOWNSEND, WASHINGTON

Printed in the United States of America

Cover art: John Schaefer, *Out Bound*, 2005. Oil on canvas, 28 x 28 inches.

Copper Canyon Press is in residence at Fort Worden State Park in Port Townsend, Washington, under the auspices of Centrum. Centrum is a gathering place for artists and creative thinkers from around the world, students of all ages and backgrounds, and audiences seeking extraordinary cultural enrichment.

LIBRARY OF CONGRESS CATALOGING-IN-PUBLICATION DATA
Jones, Richard, 1953–
The correct spelling & exact meaning / Richard Jones.
    p. cm.
ISBN 978-1-55659-317-8 (pbk. : alk. paper)
I. Title. II. Title: The correct spelling and exact meaning.
PS3560.O52475C59 2010
811'.54—dc22

                                        2009043651


98765432 FIRST PRINTING


COPPER CANYON PRESS
Post Office Box 271
Port Townsend, Washington 98368
www.coppercanyonpress.org

*for Mark Arendt*

# ACKNOWLEDGMENTS

*ABZ* "Write"

*Agni* "Rest."
  "Servants"

*American Literary Review*
  "Reveille"

*Ascent* "Dust"

*Asheville Poetry Review*
  "The Slaughter"

*Bread & Steel* "Affronts"

*The Cincinnati Review*
  "Pulchritude,"

*The Comstock Review* "My Dog as
  Auteur"

*Court Green* "King of Hearts"

*The Darfur Anthology*
  "The Lesson"
  "Revision"
  "Titles"
  "Tomorrow My Father Will
  Die"

*Diner* "The Child Lost"

*Fou* "The Pyramid"
  "Sugar?"

*Gargoyle* "Re: incarnation"
  "Walking in a Cemetery,
  My Children Ask about the
  Markings on Tombstones"

*Hiram Poetry Review* "The Way"

*Harpur Palate* "The Apple"

*Image* "Adam Praises Eve"
  "The Face"
  "The Jewel"
  "The Napkin"
  "Normal"

*JAMA* (*The Journal of the American
  Medical Association*)
  "Consent Form with
  Signature"

*The MacGuffin* "Roman Ruin"

*Narrative* "Departed"

*New Letters* "Coffee with Cream
  and Sugar"

*Onthebus* "At Last"

*Paddlefish* "Affliction"
  "Dhyana"
  "Miracles"
  "Searching for a Heart"
  "The Word in the World"

*Poet Lore* "The Plymouth"

*Poetry South* "OED"
  "This Blue World"

*Potomac Review* "The Letter *A*"

*Rock & Sling* "&"

*Smartish Pace*
  "The Seeds of Sorrow"
  "This Heaven"

*Spillway* "The Altar"
  "Confessing My Loves"
  "Fallen"
  "Polio"
  "The World Book"

*U.S. 1 Worksheets* "Toil"

*Water-Stone Review*
  "Shadowboxing"
  "The Span"

# THE CORRECT SPELLING

&

43 &

( )

!

44 ;

:

< >

45 /

–

[*sic*]

# EXACT MEANING

*they say love conquers all*
*you can't start it like a car*
*you can't stop it with a gun*

WARREN ZEVON


*My dear friend, do you see all I am saying?*

THE CLOUD OF UNKNOWING

# The Correct Spelling
# & Exact Meaning

THE CORRECT SPELLING

## OED

In the dictionary one finds the word
*lucubrate,* meaning "to study
by artificial light late at night
that one might express oneself
in writing," on the heels of *luctiferous*—
"bringing sorrow"—and this immediately
preceded by *lucrous,* which, of course, is
"pertaining to lucre" and suggests "avaricious."

To the right of *lucubrate* is *ludibrious*—
"subject of mockery"—
and the familiar *ludicrous*—
all that which is "laughably absurd."

And in the far-right column, variations
on two small words, *luff* and *lug,*
"to bring the head of a ship
nearer the wind,"
and "to pull and tug heavily and slowly,"
two tiny words that describe
what I am doing
writing at my desk late at night,
turning the pages of the dictionary to find
the correct spelling and exact meaning
of *lugubrious.*

## Rest.

It's so late I could cut my lights
and drive the next fifty miles
of empty interstate
by starlight,
flying along in a dream,
countryside alive with shapes and shadows,
but exit ramps lined
with eighteen-wheelers
and truckers sleeping in their cabs
make me consider pulling into a rest stop
and closing my eyes. I've done it in the past,
parking next to a family sleeping in a Chevy,
mom and dad up front, three kids in the back,
the windows slightly misted by the sleepers' breath.
But instead of resting, I'd smoke a cigarette,
play the radio low, and keep watch over
the wayfarers in the car next to me,
a strange paternal concern
and compassion for their well-being
rising up inside me.
This was before
I had children of my own,
and first felt the sharp edge of love
and anxiety whenever I tiptoed
into darkened rooms of sleep
to study the peaceful faces
of my beloved darlings. Now,
on lonely nights like this,
the fatherly feelings are so strong
the snoring truckers are lucky
I'm not standing on the running board,

tapping on the window,
asking, *Is everything okay?*
But it is. Everything's fine.
The trucks are all together, sleeping
on the gravel shoulders of exit ramps,
and the crowded rest stop I'm driving by
is a perfect oasis in the moonlight.
The way I see it, I've got a second wind
and an all-night country station on the radio.
Nothing for me to do on this road
but drive and give thanks:
I'll be home by dawn.

# Affronts

There are things I thoroughly dislike—
weeds, litter, graffiti, tattoos,
especially tattoos,
and any sort of firearm or weapon.
Yet no sooner do I count
and name the affronts to my sensibility
than my mind sees the many charms
of the very things I consider
utterly distasteful.
The cornflower, for instance,
that spindly yet thick-blooming blue weed
gracing the shoulders of summer roads—
I'm crazy about it, and would add its magic
to my garden, giving it a little plaque
with its name in permanent ink for all to see.
And once in the desert I saw
as in a child's drawing
a dust devil—
ornamented with bits of colorful trash,
spinning
against a perfectly blue, spotless sky.
If you'll forgive my saying this,
I've found graffiti on lonely walls
as profound and concise as poetry,
and stood beneath train trestles memorizing
the spray-painted thoughts
of some teenage prophet.
As for tattoos,
I'm sure you assume
I ponder the rose blooming on a girl's shoulder,
or the Chinese character for princess

emblazoned
on an older woman's ankle.
But no.
I'm thinking
of tattoos found in packs of gum
and my boys
who adorn their almost imperceptible biceps
with lightning bolts and hearts,
who, costumed as pirates
and armed
with wooden cap guns and shiny plastic sabers,
rend and plunder my world.

# Fallen

Tucking the kids in, I gently explain
life may be an ordeal with times of testing.
*I've* failed more times than I can count, I say.

Immediately they want to know
exactly how many times I've failed,
the precise number of grave disasters.

Wide-eyed, they fire guesses—ten?—fifteen?
No, I say, I've fallen a lot more than that.
Sixteen? A thousand? Seventeen thousand!

Well, now we're in the ballpark, I tell them,
and for a moment the three of them are
silent, as I am silent, all of us imagining

a line of resplendent catastrophes
stretching back to the day I was born.

# The Altar

I raise toward the blue of the window
a freshly sharpened pencil pointing to heaven
and blow the imperceptible dust
from the needle-tip
before taking out a clean sheet of paper
and getting down to business.
For in life's long journey
few things afford greater satisfaction
than turning the crank
and powering the cylindrical burrs
of a mechanism which sharpens
the dulled mind of a yellow No. 2 pencil.
In the silver pencil sharpener
I witness the marriage of utility and beauty
—a model for art and a purpose for life
celebrated each morning before this small altar.

# The Letter *A*

*achluophobia, acrophobia, autophobia,*
*anthophobia, apeirophobia, atephobia,*
*aulophobia, astraphobia...*

As a child I suffered
from fear of the dark,
but not from the fear of heights—

I loved climbing ladders
to sit on a rooftop,
leaping from high cliffs
into pools of still water,
or swinging from a vine
from one tree to the next.

Nor did I fear being alone;
like Wordsworth, I
welcomed the solitude
of a tiny room
or wild summer woods;
and looking back, I'm grateful
my soul had ample seedtime.

I had no fear of flowers;
as a child I imagined
nothing more wonderful
than contemplating infinity,
enthralled,
sitting on a hillside in bloom.
And had I feared the infinite,
could I have become a poet?

And because I did not fear
a building's collapse
or sweet music filling the air,
I explored the ruins of many cities
and at night in rented rooms
often fell asleep, dreaming
to a Bach fugue.

It's true:
fear of the dark
scarred me forever,
but that was a great blessing.
The compassion that fills my heart
for anyone crippled
by thunder and lightning
is unbounded—
unbounded as silence
sundered by great rolling peals of thunder
and night
hewn by lightning.

# The Lesson

I sit on a rock
at the end of the lane
waiting for the school bus
to bring my boys
home. And while I sit
I inventory thoughts
and judge most of what is
in my head
to be meaningless noise.
I shake the pebbles of the mind;
the tin can of my skull rattles.
As I sit on the rock
and listen harder, deeper,
I hum a tune
and realize it's Dylan—
*every man's conscience*
*is vile and depraved*—
and it seems I am predestined
to think of John Calvin's doctrine
of Total Depravity,
man did not merely fall
but is *born* in a fallen state
of absolute corruption and wickedness,
the dark human heart
the heart of the matter.
The tin can rattles.
I look above.
The afternoon sun
beats down on me,
unrelenting, oppressive,
and I'm tempted

to ask for freedom
from the hard thoughts a man thinks,
broken on a rock....
Then I'm broken from my reverie
by the leviathan
of the yellow bus
that rounds the corner
and spews from its belly
my children with their backpacks.
Walking the narrow lane home,
I listen to lessons
the boys learned at school.
William recites in a song
the names of the continents,
Andrew counts in Japanese
from *ichi*
to *jū,*
and together the boys insist
even I
might learn
with a small scalpel
and a pair of tweezers
how to dissect a frog
to further study the tiny heart.

## My Dog as *Auteur*

My dog is filming
the tragedy of my life,
circling this mask of sorrow
in a painfully slow tracking shot,
zooming in to capture falling tears,
lingering in close-up to show
each teardrop filled with light.

She barks when I forget lines
but licks my hand and calls me *darling*
if I get a scene just right.
We've worked together for years now—
she writing and directing,
I the star
shining brighter and brighter
in her black-and-white celluloid world.

She howls *take five*
when I can't stop crying,
then sighs, calling the day a wrap,
turning her tail to me,
going back to her doggy life—
digging in the dirt, lapping at the bowl—
knowing I will lie in bed all night
worrying my lines,
repeating them a thousand ways to the dark:
Woof. Woof. Woof.

## Pulchritude,

I fear,
is not mellifluous enough
to describe your indescribable
beauty,
so I am loath,
here on our sofa
past midnight in the dark,
to touch my lips to your ear
and whisper,
*You are the most pulchritudinous woman,*
*the most pulchritudinous in the world,*
though I am considering the possibility
that charmed by the note
of sincerity in my voice
and knowing
the children sleep,
you will close your eyes,
pull your long hair back,
and take your husband's empty hand
inside your unbuttoned blouse
to feel your beating heart,
which has never cared *which* words I choose
yet beats fast
because
you know what I'm saying.

## Roman Ruin

To repair the fallen empire of the mind,
I'd like to spend a few days
at the Raphaël

in the little Roman hotel's
quiet library,
reading book after book

devoted to the city
of eternal beauty,
its ruins and catacombs,

the history of Caesars
and lives of saints.
With my finger tracing words

I'd revel in Trastevere
or lie in the Protestant Cemetery
among graves of poets.

I'd lose myself in paintings
as I toured the Vatican's
endless hallways page by page,

or lingered over renderings
of the Last Judgment
on the Sistine Chapel's altar wall.

Chapter by chapter,
I'd note the pleasures of dining
on the Via Veneto,

the serenity of
the Tiber, the view from
the Palatine....

In the Hotel Raphaël,
left alone,
undisturbed in the library

and surrounded by books,
I'd read everything
that's been written about Rome,

and content
in my disrepair,
I'd never need to travel

beyond the lobby's fresh flowers
and open doors
to see a ruin for myself.

## Miracles

I need to witness miracles today—
a river turned to blood,
water become wine,
a burning coal touching the prophet's lips,
black ravens swooping down
to bring a starving man bread and meat,
a poor fisherman raising the dead!
I've heard theologians say
this is not the age of miracles,
but still, I'm easy to impress.
I don't need to climb out of the boat
and walk on water; I'd just like
to put my head on the pillow
while the storm still rages, and rest.

# Polio

When I was a boy, children feared
polio and the atom bomb, and we were
instructed to avoid swimming in farm ponds
and to turn our gaze from the brilliant
flash in the sky. They also taught us
to fear communism, but I *liked* the idea
of sharing what we have on this earth—
washing machines, bicycles, wool hats.
It seemed to me a person's birthright
to have a roof and food and one day off.
At school, stationed by the teacher's desk,
I faced the faces of my classmates and read
my midterm report, "Utopian Visions."

I never pretended, never kidded myself
communism could make us all equal.
Our classmate, Jessie—once the swiftest
on the playground—returned one summer
slowed by leg braces and metal crutches.
The teacher didn't fail Jessie when,
too sick to write a report, a struggle
just to rise and stand before the class,
Jessie did nothing more than ask us all
to turn and look out the windows.
"Imagine first," she said, "the mighty blast.
And then—over the land—the mushroom cloud."

# The World Book

While hungry men huddled
in the wind-ravaged street
and waited in line at the church
for the food pantry doors to open,
I counted myself lucky
(when not working double shifts),
to spend time in the thrift store,
searching the dusty chaos
of ramshackled bookshelves
for out-of-print poetry
hidden among obsolete textbooks
and discarded Bibles.
Finding nothing, I'd kneel
to read on the lowest sagging shelf
a set of the twenty-volume
*World Book Encyclopedia,*
picking up "P" to look up *poverty,*
or "A" to look up *alcoholism.*
While others thrilled to find
a good pair of winter boots
or a shiny toaster oven, I'd try
to reckon all the many things
I didn't know, and find an answer,
turning to "M" to contemplate
*misery* and *miracle,* "H" to consider *heaven.*
I found the *World Book* endlessly
diverting, but longed for epiphanies,
and often surprised myself
(since I wasn't a believer)
leaving those thrift stores perfectly content,
nothing in my arms save a Bible

purchased for a dime, a quarter.
I bought leather Bibles in every translation—
King James, New Living, American—
most of the volumes untouched, the spines unbroken.
Today they line the shelves of my study.
The vintage Bible I'm reading today
I found in a thrift store in Duluth,
next to the Red Horse, a tavern I frequented.
A pristine white leather volume,
I love its little gold cross attached to a zipper
that when unzipped
reveals the Scripture's gold-leaf edges
fresh as the day they were printed,
the paper unblemished as the lamb.
The frontispiece still bears,
in the perfect cursive of another age,
a mother's inscription:
*To my little daughter,*
*This is one book you will always read.*
When I see the untouched bright pages,
I remember the Bibles on the thrift store shelves,
the other inscribed Bibles
that I never bought
because they were *too* dog-eared,
too tattered, stained, or broken,
the pages falling out like an old man's teeth—
used Bibles whose poetry had been read,
the words consumed every day like bread.

# Shadowboxing

*You are the shadow, the shadow is you,*
William says as we walk home from the pool
in wet bathing suits, shadowboxing.
It's the sort of thing he says now and then,
a koan, the Zen wisdom of his six-year-old mind.
And of course what he has observed, or rather,
the enlightened perspective he is wont to teach
his increasingly absentminded, unseeing father,
is both true and useful, and I am suddenly ashamed
of the little regard I've had for my own shadow,
constant companion that stretches arms wide across
late-afternoon lawns, looms at night on alley walls,
or melts into nothing to hide from the noonday sun.
I would ask him to teach me more, but when we
stop on the corner, waiting to cross with the light,
I look down at the child's shadow beside the man's:
William's small arms hooking and jabbing, two fists
knocking some sense into the darkness of his father's head.

## Toil

I see my mother years ago in the South
as she turns soil, plants seed, weeds the beds,
pours and carries the precious water, dirt
smudging an alabaster cheek, long black hair
under a straw hat, happy. But did my mother
really fill a watering can, or ever like a sentry
walk the perimeter of our house? I remember
muddy gloves, a rusting green-handled trowel.
And, planted in hard dirt by the redbrick house,
spindly, stalk-thin zinnias stoical as prisoners
standing in the sun and suffering the sentence
of long southern summers, my mother's zinnias
undeniably beautiful, because flowers just *are*,
even under the most difficult, adverse conditions.

## Tomorrow My Father Will Die

I'm watching television with my daughter, who loves children's
shows that spell out words—*behind... beyond... become.* She asks what
each word means, words that to her father are heralds divining the
future or reports from the forgotten past. The letters on the screen
are lifted up by wise owls and friendly tigers. It is like a dream, the
way the word *being* blows apart, the letters drifting away like
scattered dust and ash. *Believe. Belong.* On the television screen I see
the ghost of my reflection, a face old and haggard. Then I see the
appointed day ahead. We are sitting by my father's grave, his grand-
daughter and I joined by the animals and the letters. The animals
are silent and the letters spell nothing, but because she loves to
read, my daughter climbs onto my lap and opens the well-thumbed
black book to the ribbon-marked page of psalms—

> *the wind blows, and we are gone—*
> *as though we had never been here.*

## The Plymouth

In a corner of a field, at the edge of an old wood,
a tire-less automobile, abandoned in mud and weeds
to rust and crumble, befriended me the saddest year
of childhood. While my cousins walked to school,
I'd let the screen door slam behind me, and run
through town to the abandoned farm where,
doorless, the black car waited. I'd climb inside
and spin the dead speedometer's defeated arrow,
imagining life's endless road unfolding, beckoning.
I could hear the engine roar and purr, waiting for me
to put the car in gear. I'd grip the big steering wheel
and drive somewhere exotic, like Sheboygan or
Green Bay. This was long ago, in Savannah,
where I'd never seen a snowflake or a frozen lake,
when the world was still a place to be imagined
rather than remembered, as I remembered it today,
when the caravan of classic cars rolled slowly past,
and I spotted my good old friend, the big-fendered
1940 Plymouth, proudly waxed and shining, piloted
by a grinning white-haired man in a blue sports cap
who looked just like me, and waved as he passed.

## The Span

I, too, could live alone,
pacing that narrow windowsill,
black wings spanned across my back,
and pondering the brevity of days,

looking out the window,
never leaving the light;
and I would pray that when I die,
and like a fly am found dead on the sill—

wings iridescent in the sun—
someone will lift me up,
perhaps with a white sheet of paper
on which a poem of joy is written,

a poem someone will read
as I'm carried to the trash and thrown away.

# The Way

*a farmer pulling radishes*
*pointed the way with a radish*

ISSA

I had been driving
cross-country for days,
the miles hard fought
as if the soul had been
tossed out the window,
a last cigarette, red embers
exploding in the rearview
mirror, as if the heart, too,
were dead but still thinking
it would see tomorrow,
the engine of the mind racing,
a dangerous machine,
the eyes hard as flint,
the highway's open mouth
yawning all night, swallowing
despair and doubt, my
foot on the gas, hand
on the wheel, the needle
racing, headlights searching,
the dawn coming up a stranger
and the sun at noon offering
absolutely nothing, and then
atop a clear green hillside pasture—
I sped past them in a heartbeat—
three white crosses, a farmer's way
of telling me the road I was on
and where the hell I was going.

## Affliction

My wife the doctor
says I exaggerate
when, in bed, ice pack on my head,
I describe my symptoms—
my sore throat *burning razors,*
the flu *a foreign army occupying the country of my body,*
a high fever *the fires of hell.*

She rolls her eyes at apocalyptic metaphors,
but I've read that in the hospital
many patients find no words
to describe their pain
or say in plain English how they feel.
To silence all hyperbole,
she puts a thermometer in my mouth

even though I've not *begun*
to communicate what's going on
in the universe of my body—
hot pokers behind the eyes,
pyrotechnics in the temporal lobes,
the mind's machinery pounding
like a stamp mill in a steel foundry.

My wife holds the thermometer
up close to her face to read the bad news—
*the world holds its breath—*
then shakes it clear
and claims I'm "normal."
She takes my wrist and looks at her watch,
but it's too late—

I'm dying.
Nothing left to do
but open the barn door of speech
and loose every danger and trouble—
the sun turning black as sackcloth,
the full moon bloodred,
the stars of the sky falling to the earth,

and a moseying cow—oblivious to the end—
mindlessly chewing cud.

# The Slaughter

After her child died and was buried,
my sister stood in my farmhouse kitchen,
leaning on the scarred wooden table.
Exposed shelves were lined with glass jars—
canned beets, tomatoes, and peaches—
like painted saints who intercede for us
on the walls of silent, empty churches.
I drank a glass of cold well water,
metallic and bitter, the taste of loneliness.
The sky in the window was cold and blue.
The house, inside, was cold and blue.
Later, I paced the study's bookshelves,
unable to think, unable not to think.
My sister sat, keeping her own counsel.
The books turned their faces from my grief,
but like old friends stood watchful by me.
There was no one else. Outside we heard
voices, the landlord farmer and his two boys,
the grind of the tractor pulling the flatbed
carrying cattle. Inside, all day, the house was
cold and blue. In the evening the windows
grew black. My sister climbed the stairs
to sleep in a room tucked under the eaves.
That night, the stars abandoned their sky
to form a perfect canopy above her bed.
Knowing she would be sleepless for many winters,
I was grateful for the nearness of her heaven.
Downstairs, sitting alone in the dark, I listened
to her stars whisper stories of light and hope
as the cattle were led lowing to slaughter.

# The Child Lost

*for my nephew, Andrew, 1978–1984*

Twenty-five years ago,
the car pulled to the side of the road
in the middle of the night,
the door opened,
and without saying goodbye
you climbed out. A five-year-old boy,
you stood there, quiet and still
in the rearview mirror, growing
smaller as the car traveled on,
speeding through towns,
your family carried
through cities that frightened them.
They longed to stop,
but they were mere passengers,
without volition,
and the dark journey was all,
and all they'd ever know—
wheels forever turning,
empty road rolling
to blue horizons and beyond.
Though they could imagine
home lights burning,
the car arriving,
passengers safe,
and you, the lost child,
a man now grown,
waiting in the open door
to greet them.

# The Face

*Emmett Till's mother*
*speaking over the radio*

In a comforting voice the mother tells
what it was like to touch her dead boy's face.

She'd lingered and traced
the broken jaw, the crushed eyes,

the face *that* badly beaten, disfigured,
before confirming his identity.

And then she compares his face to
the face of Jesus, dying on the cross.

This woman says no, she'd not recognize
her Lord, for He was beaten far, far worse

than her son, whom she loved with all her heart.
For she could still discern her son's curved earlobe,

but the face of Christ, she said,
was beaten by the whole world.

# Write

Write as if you were proclaiming
from a pulpit to believers who
have ears to listen and eyes to see
a parable's riches, prayer's might.
Write from the heart, knowing
the heart is deceitful and full of lies,
knowing your heart has been broken,
emptied, so that the Lord in His mercy
could fill it with His joy. Trust God—
rise like a feather on the wind. Be
guided by the spirit, the same spirit that
groans as it lifts and carries your burdens.
Write poems because you have been shattered,
because poetry is sacred and holy, because
a poem left unwritten dies and you become
a walking tomb, a whitewashed sepulcher.

## Searching for a Heart

Last Tuesday
I stumbled into the classroom
as though I'd been shot—
face pale, hand on my heart.
I staggered to the head of the table.
Waiting students opened journals,
observed and took notes
as with a knife I cut
the bullet from my chest.
Between finger and thumb
I held the misshapen piece of lead
like a diamond
for all to see,
then dropped the bloody bullet
into a tin pan with a
*clink.*
Taking roll,
checking off names,
I cleaned the blade on my pant leg,
placed the knife back in my jacket,
and asked if anyone had a watch
I could borrow
to manage the next fifty minutes.
I began the lecture
with a question for the class:
"Who knows a word
that rhymes with
*clink*?"
Hands went up—
"Ink," "Blink," "Wink," "Zinc,"
"Link"...

As Time hammered nails in a coffin,
the students helped their wounded teacher,
and together we searched
for the perfect word
with the exact meaning I needed.

# Adam Praises Eve

*for Laura*

She is so beautiful, it is enough—
her skin zinc-
white, like milk,
her nipples like cherries,
hair a long night without stars.
I find irresistible the ink
of the blue vein
pulsing above her left ankle,
the green of those intelligent eyes,
the sly wink.
Everything she wants, I want,
and though my mind is cleaved,
my full heart can only rejoice.
The apple snaps under my teeth—
a glad sound, like the link
of a chain breaking.
She reaches for me. I blink
and am suddenly ashamed,
but with original love
she takes my hand and leads me,
broken and free, out of the garden.

# Normal

*tent revival, 1957*

My mother squeezed my hand as they led the preacher to the stage. *When things get back to normal, God will put on black robes*—through the speakers the old man's voice, though he looked frail, rose and thundered—*and ascend to the mercy seat to judge the world, the ruined cities, the devastated hills, the living and the risen dead. When things get back to normal, He'll open the Book of Life and read what each man has done, said, and written, reciting our words and deeds to the angels to see if there was forgiveness like honey on our tongues. When things get back to normal, all will stand in final judgment*—I could see the tent lights shining in my mother's eyes—*and be burned like dead branches or blessed with the incomprehensible fire of mercy. When things get back to normal, we will kneel before the throne of heaven, old things will pass away, and at last we will be restored to the meaning and purpose of all creation, and God will be our God. Until then*—white moths swirling overhead in strings of tent lights—*He will pour out his spirit on all people, your sons and daughters will prophesy, your old men will dream dreams, and your young men will see visions.*

&

little piece of string
binding
devil & saint,
salvation & ruin


( )

wisdom hidden from the wise
whispered through cupped hands


!

tiny mustard seed
and faith's green shoot rising
heavenward
to bloom

;

buoy in the channel;
no, it's the swimmer,
head lifted for air


:

head on a pillow,
eyes wide open


< >

what he wrote with his finger in the dirt

/

the virgule,
as in
"the soldier's spear / piercing the heart"


—


on headstones:
the life


[*sic*]


knowledge
of the original error

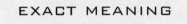

EXACT MEANING

## This Heaven

How wonderful to stand in plaid pajamas in the early morning light drinking the first cup of coffee as my daughter learning to ride her new yellow bike sails up and down the block while neighborhood children one by one appear on scooters or skates greeting each other as they always do with shouts and salutations sailing over the last summer flowers and dew-drenched lawns which their barefooted parents tiptoe across to say *good morning* to say *isn't this heaven* to stand in the lane in awe every child playing until Sarah stops her bike beside me and asks me to bend down for a kiss I think but no she wants the pink purse hanging from my shoulder which she'll take on the school bus and suddenly all the children are gone the bus chugging down the lane and I'm left alone rolling my daughter's tiny bicycle down the suddenly empty suddenly terribly quiet lane.

## Consent Form with Signature

She says if she loses her legs
she will be okay:
she will focus on immediate rewards—
learning alone
to drop from bed to wheelchair,
dressing,
using the bathroom.
Her mind,
her intelligence
are undiminished,
and the zeppelin of imagination
unmoored from the ground of the body
—ascendant. She's not waiting—
the path of grace might be faster on wheels.

# Titles

The Lost Son,
published in 1948,
is full of poems
I love—
"Moss-Gathering,"
"Big Wind,"
"My Papa's Waltz,"
"Flower Dump."
Roethke's titles alone—
Words for the Wind,
Praise to the End!—
inscribe the mind,
inscribe the heart
with echoing cries
of stone, leaves, roots, wind.
In 1953,
the year I was born,
The Waking
contained the beautiful
"Elegy for Jane,"
a poem I needed
again this morning
to heal.

# The Apple

I pare an apple for my little girl, stunning,
as usual, in a shimmering Cinderella gown.
I cut seven shining crescent moons
to array and serve on a deep blue plate,
and recall the skill needed to cut
and remove the hide of a white-tailed deer.

Before Sarah was born, before I imagined
her in my life or how life would change,
I met in rural Wisconsin an insurance adjuster.
His hobby was taxidermy. Headless carcasses,
waiting to be skinned and butchered,
hung from pulley ropes in the trees.

I visited the taxidermist with my carpenter friend.
We borrowed a pulley and winch to hoist
a plate-glass window to the second story
of an old house we were renovating.
It was brilliant, sparkling autumn. Deer season.
Gunshots and church bells rang in the distance.

What I recall most vividly is the teenage girl
who lived in the house next door to the taxidermist.
Barefoot in a sunlit Sunday dress, maple leaves swirling
on the lawn, she danced, pale and long-limbed,
practicing baton twirls, throwing the metal bar
high in the air, catching it with a curtsy.

Enchanted, I steadied myself
against my friend's truck, watching the silver baton
spinning crosses in the air. I remember that
as if it were yesterday. That, and the cold stare

the girl's father gave me as he stood on the porch,
knife in hand, paring an apple.

# Epithalamium

*for Anthony and Marianne*

I tell my students I don't have the wisdom
to explain beauty and mystery, and most days
I know I don't know much about anything,
and will be held accountable for teaching
those who hope to gain some small
insight into the inscrutability of this world;
yet I know the real heart of things, the love
we lack and must rekindle, will not be found by
taking notes or reading past midnight; love is
incarnational, born in the grace-filled hour when,
the book closed, a wife climbs the stairs to join
her husband, that young student who suffered
beside her through school as if lashed to his desk,
his eyes on her as he waited for the lesson to end.

## The Seeds of Sorrow

We're taught by the seers
that the seeds of sorrow
are sown in the moment
of joy;
nonetheless,
it's bliss to wander
hand in hand
with my little daughter
through the summer-glad garden
while the sun windmills
through the verdant, latticed branches.
Unhurried by time,
we follow a tranquil path of stones
which twists and turns through weeping
cherries, poplars, and pines.
She says hello to the blue bunting
sipping at the birdbath,
discovers angels
purchased from the garden center
and hidden among delphiniums
and hollyhocks—
cherubs
smaller than she.
Even in winter,
when fragile veils of snow
lift from sleeping flowerbeds
to blow and dance like spirits
beneath winterkill-branches,
we don't go in the house—
we listen in the quiet
to the crunch of our boots in frozen snow,

and holding gloved hands
we walk on
beneath a desolate sky
that blazes like a wounded heart.
Then we stand
motionless
and look up,
watching heaven
ignite its ancient stars—
those cold and distant fires
that discover to us nothing
but labyrinths of darkness—
and I hold her hand tighter.

# King of Hearts

*a letter to my father*

Though you are gone,
I found you today
lying free and lonely
under the table, unseen
among the scattered toys,

even though I ceaselessly
warn your grandchildren
*not to lose a single card,*
knowing they'll want them all
when they gather to play.

Kneeling, I saw your face—
the sword and the crown—
and did not return the card to the pack,
but slipped it in my shirt pocket,
and patted my heart for luck.

## Sugar?

I don't like talking as much as I used to,
which I mean in both senses—
that I no longer enjoy "talking,"
and that I use fewer words,
averse to the few I manage.

Perhaps I am becoming more inward,
more solipsistic, that is, if one *can* become
more solipsistic; I mean, after all, solipsism
is a state of being, an either/or condition.
I mean, lately I feel that I'm the only one

who could possibly know what I mean
when I try to say something meaningful.
For instance, this morning at the coffee shop
(in what started in line as a casual
conversation about the weather),

I *attempted* to articulate the nuances of a thought
to a stranger, to *share* an epiphany's lightning,
only to find myself—like young Keats—dying,
standing alone on the shore of the world,
letting all thought sink into nothingness.

Then the stranger in line asked, "What's solipsism?"
Then the kid behind the counter said, "Sugar?"

# Departed

I just this moment
noticed on my desk
my elegant father's
silver tie clip, thin
as a dash announcing
a sudden revelation.
The flat silver bar,
meant to be engraved,
my father chose
to leave untouched,
spartan and spare
being more his style,
like a poet who gives
silence its due. How
did it come to rest,
mute on my cluttered desk?
I must have placed it here
last year, when he died,
thinking its presence
would reassure me,
thinking a silver tie clip
symbolized something
that could never be
expressed in a poem,
something sacred I might
examine for meaning,
as I examine it now,
wishing my father
had thought to engrave
a motto, or his initials,
then suddenly discovering,

as if he'd just now
taken off the tie clip,
placed it on my desk,
and departed the room,
something far better—
the ghostly whorls
of my father's
fingerprints.

# OMG

*unless you change*
*and become like little children*

The Buddha
didn't have a cell phone,
Jesus
didn't listen to an iPod,
and Emily Dickinson
never once checked her e-mail;
that said,
I confess I wouldn't mind being interrupted
by Beethoven's Ninth Symphony
(my personal ringtone)
and listening to
a prerecorded message from the Buddha,
an unfinished sermon on suffering
with an 800 number to call if
I am interested in enlightenment.
And you can bet that for ninety-nine cents
I'd download all the flutes and lyres
that played for Jesus
when he dined in the homes
of tax collectors and sinners.
And each day
it would be like salvation itself
to open my e-mail
and find
*bulletins from immortality.*
I know Issa and Bashō,
who quicken the heart
with a chiseled thought,
never dreamed of text messaging

the way my children do—
inventing a new language
and furiously typing with their thumbs
as if their lives depended on it—
but nonetheless
I am telling the truth:
if that's what it takes
to hold pure poetry in my hand,
if that's what's required
to enter the kingdom,
I'll put down my pens and books
and turn from my endless study.
I'll become like a child
waiting to decipher
text messages from God.

# The Jewel

I like this moment when there is nothing
more I need to do,
when I have emptied
everything on the conveyor—
eggs, bread, apples, and some chocolate
I will give my children after homework—
and I am free to study
the checkout lady's red face
ever so slightly gasping for air,
the quick hands of the teenage boy
distractedly bagging groceries,
and the lady behind me so tiny
she stands on tiptoes to empty her cart.
I have all the time in the world
to open my wallet and set aside bills
for the Salvation Army bell ringer
standing outside the automatic glass doors
in the dark and falling snow,
time even to survey the sad
faces on the magazines
and read the headlines and confessions
and forgive each star by name.
But when everything has been counted
and bagged, the bill calculated
and the receipt handed to me,
I've forgotten where I am and what I'm doing,
so determined am I to see the angels
William Blake tells me
stand among us,
cherubim lingering by the illuminated
bins of produce,

seraphim protecting the fish sticks
in the frozen-food section.
The cashier is saying, "Sir? Sir?"
but now I am seeking to pierce the veil
that separates us from the saints in heaven.
Gazing out over the rows of shoppers
waiting in lines with their carts,
and now holding up everyone in line behind me,
I am squinting to find my father, who loved fish sticks,
to see him in his appointed place
among the multitudes of angels and saints,
the heavenly choirs
I can almost hear
singing to me.

# Coffee with Cream and Sugar

I know a man should like it best
when he rises before the sun
and makes coffee. It makes me
think of horses and ranches,
a time when the wide world
seemed boundless and possible.

Yet I've long preferred waking
to the sweet song of your voice
saying, "Here's your coffee."
That's all. By the time I open
one eye, you've already gone.

Pillows piled high, I sit awhile.
From the night table I lift my cup.
Each morning the same sweet favor
and routine. I'm slow to leave dreams,
and who can blame me? It's warm
in bed, and you might come back.

## Confessing My Loves

Just as I love bookstores,
I love liquor stores,
slowly browsing aisles
marked Gin or Wine,
taking the time to savor
the array of choices
just as I do in bookstores
when I wander aisles
marked Fiction or History,
Metaphysics and Art.
Like books,
liquor can take a lifetime to make—
the skills of the champagne maker
handed down
through generations
of a noble house.
And just as it's one of life's pleasures
to hold a cloth- or leather-covered
book in the hands,
it's gratifying
to heft the bottle's sculpted shape—
towering spires, homely carafes,
squat jugs wrapped in wicker,
and some like potable treasure
in ornate boxes with crystal glasses.
When one lifts bottles to the light
to behold the color—
cut-grass green of crème de menthe,
amber of Cointreau,
the transparency of pure rum or white tequila,
the red clouds of tawny port—

it's hard not to think
of ranks of books
with richly colored bindings.
As the lonely scholar
or bibliophile
esteems and reveres
a Shakespeare folio
or a Gutenberg Bible,
the oenologist
dreams
of a year when summer was perfect—
nothing but yellow sun all day
warming the earth.
What can be more satisfying
than a bottle retrieved from time's cellar,
a wine so transcendent
a man would think
he is drinking
with the bride and groom at Cana?
When I leave a bookstore
my bookbag's heavy
with hardcovers
and paperbacks,
and I always need a box
to carry from the liquor store
all my new loves and treasures safely
home, where each night
I browse the library,
sipping a glass of sherry
Baudelaire would have relished
and remembering
the summer I was twelve
when I sneaked my first taste
of Father's bourbon,

the summer I became aware
of the glory of
the novel.
*War and Peace.*
*Great Expectations.*
Reading perfected
childhood's loneliness,
and at bedtime
it was impossible
to turn out the light:
I'd stay up all night,
turning pages,
reading past dawn—
*The Grapes of Wrath,*
*The Sun Also Rises*—
reading until I'd hear
my mother
stirring from bed,
then padding downstairs
to cook breakfast.
Over a cup of strong black coffee,
with first light
shining in through the windows,
I'd sit at the kitchen table
and tell my mother everything I'd read,
everything.

# Revision

I choose to believe that on holiday from London's deadly soot and fog with their little daughter in the south of France, and without the remotest conception that a committee of translators had long been working to bring into submission the many errors of the King James Bible, "the noblest monument of English prose," my mother and father were inspired to conceive a child on September 30, 1952, unknowingly celebrating, as farmers harvested hillside vineyards, the publication in America of the Revised Standard Version, a model of accuracy, clarity, and euphony, a red pew Bible whose depths their grown son would one day plumb with prayers for illumination.

# Dhyana

*A monk can witness this*
*for himself*

BUDDHA, *SAMADHANGA SUTTA*

Walks are solitary journeys
of mind and spirit
best practiced
by a temperament as serene
and composed
as the austere grounds
of a many-chambered mountain monastery;
and though I understand this,
I welcome and enjoy
my boys' company and companionship.
For just as dogs
complement and complete any excursion,
my two young sons enrich and perfect my aimlessness.
Like dogs, my boys say little,
intent only on moving forward,
even though, like dogs,
they tend to run ahead on the crushed stones,
paths that wend through acres
of meadows and woods,
searching thickets of hyssop and larkspur,
disappearing like shadows into green
banks of azalea and rhododendron.
But a public garden has rules,
an etiquette to be observed.
In stern tones, I shout their names—
*Andrew! William!*—
ordering them out of flowerbeds,

commanding them to walk like gentlemen.
And often, as if in recompense
for some future rebelliousness
they have yet to conceive or commit,
they do walk like gentlemen,
and like robed monks
silently cross the arching bridge
to Sansho-En,
the Garden of Three Islands.
On a rocky switchback path by a falling stream
we ascend to a hilltop temple.
At narrow bamboo gates, we bow.
Inside silent walls
by a raked sea of sun-bleached pebbles,
we sit in calm meditation. We breathe.
For maybe two or three minutes,
the boys are as single-minded as Tu Fu or Li Po,
studying raked rocks and sculpted pines,
imagining wind on water,
two little Buddhas
refusing to mourn
the transience of all things.
Sometimes we make up poems together,
and without prompting,
William adjusts his posture
and recites to the sky—

> *Peace is warm—*
> *sounds like crickets*
> *and looks like the ocean*

—then Andrew tosses back his hair from his eyes
and says to the sun,

*Japanese garden—*
*water rushing down the stones—*
*breeze and peaceful day*

Then
the day's peace passes
and the boys' mood changes
as a cloud's moving shadow
apparently
gives the boys permission
to behave like dogs again,
to dash down the hillside
startling birds
and a pair of little old ladies
at the foot of the bridge.
Bright laughter
ringing over the water,
the boys vanish behind pillars of trees.
The Buddha says enlightened monks
can pass unimpeded through stone walls,
and walk on water without sinking
as if walking on dry land.
But boys, too, can do this,
and like winged birds
Andrew and William fly through the air
to touch the sun and moon
before running back up the path
to roll in the grass
and wrestle by the temple gate,
where their father sits, serene, composed,
quelled in his soul and lamenting nothing,
enraptured by this heavenly world
to which he bears witness.

# Re: incarnation

In the next life, I want to return
as a storied football coach,
a Grand Prix champion,
the decathlon's gold medalist;

or a pool shark,
traveling with cue
from town to town, hall to hall,
fleecing marks with a mercenary heart;

or maybe it would be interesting
to ride the rails,
heading nowhere,
sleeping in aspen groves quaking beneath the stars;

or maybe as the black-suited undertaker
devoting a life
to the consoling art
of grooming dead bodies;

or his brother,
the gravedigger, who—
as carefully as the sculptor carves the body
from a block of pure white marble—

carves
with his backhoe
perfect rectangles
in the hard black earth.

## This Blue World

When I was a boy, my father was forever
asking if I was
"checked-out with the controls."
"Are you checked-out with the controls?"
Before I would undertake
the smallest task—
hammering a nail,
turning a screw,
polishing my shoes—
or when I embarked on the most modest mission—
going to school in the morning
or grabbing my glove to play baseball
in a field near our house
in the failing light
of an August evening—
he'd ask the same question:
"Are you checked-out with the controls?"
As a boy, I understood his meaning,
the urgency of my father's instruction.
A decorated Army Air Corps pilot,
my father flew over the "hump,"
and looked down on the Himalayas.
"It was," he said,
"like spending an hour near God."
The controls meant the electrical panel,
the oxygen pressure gauge and flow indicator,
the cowl flap handles,
and windshield de-icing control valve handle
in the cockpit of a C-47.
It was exhilarating,
and a little terrible,

74

the way a skillful captain,
heedless of weather
and black bursts of flak,
could lift heavy loads
into the air above the earth.
The cloudless day we buried my father—
*a perfect day for flying*—
I gave thanks at graveside
for the lesson the captain tried to teach the boy,
the miracle that was my father's life,
and his hope
that I safely fly through this blue world
knowing the terror of wings, the sweet gift of flight.

# The Napkin

When it comes to conversation,
I like the idea
of the Wailing Wall,

scribbling a petition
on a scrap of paper
and slipping the paper scrap

into a crack
between sun-blistered stones,
knowing our prayers may not be granted

but trusting the silence that answers.
I'm a long way from Jerusalem
and the temple,

but believe
the Holy of Holies is
always near,

even in the all-night diner where
people gather, talking in smoky booths
while I, a lonely supplicant,

write petitions on white napkins
pulled from the shiny dispenser—
little prayers I pen and leave under dirty plates.

I assume my note is removed
just like the many prayers left in the temple wall
are removed by

devout caretakers
who silently carry the paper scraps into the desert
and bury them by the hundreds in the sand

and wonder when I leave
what the Portuguese dishwasher thinks
when he buses the table,

glancing
at a prayer written
in a language he cannot understand.

## Walking in a Cemetery, My Children Ask about the Markings on Tombstones

Roses—
the brevity of earthly existence.
And flying birds—the flight of the soul.

*

Willows symbolize earthly sorrow,
the butterfly
an early death.

*

The hourglass with wings of time,
a candle snuffed, a broken column
—mortality, loss, and mourning.

*

An open book denotes a teacher;
a tree stump with ivy,
the head of family.

*

A handshake says farewell.
An urn ablaze is
undying friendship.

*

Trumpeters herald the Resurrection,
portals are the passageway
to the eternal journey,

*

and thistles,
like those growing wild in our flowerbeds,
are for remembrance.

# Dust

*I will repay you*
*for the years the locusts have eaten*

I

I'd set the sprinkler
to water the dying lilacs,
and come inside
to lie on my bed's white comforter
and rest,

so exhausted
was I with the effort
to cross the desert
I'd made of life.
That summer,

the drought
had been a godsend:
I'd found
a familiar comfort
whenever I surveyed

the once-green
neighborhood's plain
of yellowed grasses,
or paused to commiserate
with sulking flowers
hanging their heads
so low.

2

As I said,
I'd set the sprinkler,
climbed
the stairs to the bedroom
and closed my eyes,

but every few seconds
the highest drops
of the sprinkler's metronome
splattered the window
like the promised rain,

and I felt
compelled
to open my eyes
as each sun-blessed drop
burned slowly down—

tiny rivers
cleansing
the dry dust of the pane.
Lying on the bed, eyes closed,
I felt compelled to look—
*to rend my heart*—
but didn't.

## The Pyramid

Last night, when I woke at 4 a.m.,
I tried to calculate the amount
of wine I've consumed in my life,
a bottle a day for forty years,
then tried to reckon the mass
of empty bottles laid side by side,
stacked in the shape of a pyramid;
in the darkened room I imagined
the sun coming up and shining
through the blue and green glass,
the sunlight a fire blazing inside
each bottle, the towering pyramid
perfectly radiant and eternally burning
in the desert of my mind, like a god.

# Servants

I wouldn't mind a house
managed by servants—
an English butler
to advise me
whether to take tea in the study
or outside in the garden,
a cook whose kitchen is a temple
and whose table bears testimony
to imagination and love,
a gardener to tend the hedges
of the children's boxwood labyrinth,
a housekeeper who brings order
to the library's scattered books,
and most important of all,
a secretary and amanuensis,
an angel who, unseen, leaves
each morning on my desk
a ream of fresh paper
and an onyx fountain pen
beside a little silver bell
I might lift and ring
to summon all twelve muses
if it is they whom I want,
if I thought they ever had
something poetic to say.

# Reveille

When I went home to visit my sister
in the stone house by the river,
I couldn't sleep, and so I rose early,
before dawn, and entered the quiet
temple of the living room to sit
in simple meditation. Palms up,
legs crossed, shoulders squared,
I took a minute to relax my body,
then began to count slow breaths,
attentive to the task of emptying
the merest thought from the mind,
as if sweeping cobwebs from corners.
Moment by moment my heart grew
calm. The windows filled with light
and birdsong announced the morning.
Out of nothingness, light and birdsong.
With eyelids almost closed, I imagined
a peaceful sky free of drifting clouds—
heaven's immaculate, eternal blue.
As I sat, time passed, like the river
quickened by wind. Sun-diamonds
sparkled on wind-shirred water,
and all around the house red azaleas
blossomed, burning like a fiery moat
as towering pines swayed high above.
Perfectly still, quietly alert, I sat
and I breathed—the mind balanced.
Then I heard the soft yet distinct
notes of a distant trumpet.
I did not move, or open my eyes,
but only listened—yes, a trumpet.

The soaring notes entered my being.
My first thought was of angels on high—
the Lord coming on clouds of glory.
But the next instant brought the truth:
not a trumpet, but a bugle—a soldier
at the fort upriver, sounding reveille.
How could I have forgotten the fort,
having grown up among soldiers and war?
How could I have forgotten the battlements,
the armaments I've known since childhood?
And so like my father, a soldier,
I rose to defend the day,
to praise the light in song
like any bird or poet,
knowing this could be the very day
when angels blow their trumpets
and wake everyone.

# The Word in the World

Death knows where to find me—
sitting in the study past midnight,
reading the dictionary by lamplight,
searching for meanings, nuances, origins.
I could spend eternity
marveling at the art of syllabication,
pronouncing syllables into the night,
my lips obediently following
the slashes and symbols
of the International Phonetic Alphabet.
All night I look for the obsolete words
preceded by a dagger
or foreign phrases in bold italics,
frowning at anything "derogatory,"
blushing at anything "vulgar,"
at anything verging on the "obscene."
I find it reassuring
words have more than one spelling,
and am astonished
by breath's symphony of sounds—
fricatives, liquids, and plosives,
the cries of stresses
and the whisper of sibilants.
And—elusive as wind—
the optional sounds,
sometimes pronounced, sometimes not
(and always enclosed within round brackets).
Old English, Middle English, Old French,
Late Latin. Colloquial, poetic, slang, archaic.
I can lose myself in a word like *bat*,
"to wink or flutter,"

as in, "bat one's eyelashes,"
which is probably a variation of *bate*,
in falconry meaning
"to flap the wings wildly."
The chronology of homonyms!
The transitivity of verbs!
Deep into the dead-silent night I read,
loving the dictionary's illustrative quotations,
the clarifying phrases that bring to life
the phenomenal world in simple words—
*rain* or *disciple*—as in Shakespeare's
"The rain it raineth every day."
Or Saint John's witness to the Resurrection:
"Then were the disciples glad, when they saw the Lord."

## At Last

I gather my three young children to ready them for bed. We climb the stairs, armed with plastic swords, rifles, magic wands. In our tiny bathroom, I help the children with their nightly ablutions and tooth brushings. Our ritual involves bubblegum-flavored toothpaste, much frothy spitting, and loud gargling. Andrew and William open their mouths wide—like lions—and I bravely put my head inside to examine every tooth. Sarah—balanced like a ballerina on her step—simply smiles, and I am delight's mirror when she lifts her chin to show her white teeth. Then in the hall the children undress—three fountains tossing clothes in the air.

Much attention is paid to the habiliments of night. In their bedrooms the children furtively bedeck and festoon themselves for sleeping while I divine the answer to the riddle, "What pajamas are we wearing?" They tell me to wait in my bedroom. They huddle in the hall while I call out the myriad possibilities: "Tight-fitting long johns with spaceships and planets? Pink Princess footie pj's with zipper?" "Nope, guess again!" "Black silk pajamas embroidered with red dragons? Cinderella's sequined ball gown?" When I am empty of guesses, the children parade triumphantly into the room sporting basketball uniforms and cowboy hats, or modeling spiffy plaid button-pajamas with matching robes and slippers.

Atop my bed, they circle like puppies until they find perfect bliss. When voices quiet, I open the evening's book and read. Snuggled together, rapt, we attend to the mystery of words rising as dreams. They are quiet as snow in a meadow at night. They are pure listening. Sometimes we pontificate upon truth and love, but always go back to our book, flying to distant galaxies, or walking the earth with dinosaurs. Sarah—tricked by a toad or kissed by a prince— soon closes her eyes; I carry her to her bed and tuck her in with her pink pony. William snuggles deeper, burrowing into his pillow, falling into a deep and profound sleep. Immovable object, he will slumber undisturbed until morning.

Andrew, the oldest, if allowed, would remain awake all night, his eyes bright, like stars. But I usher him to his room and up the bunk bed's ladder to his perch at the top where, after prayers and kisses, he'll read an hour longer. He puts on a miner's helmet and turns on its light; in the dark room, light beams from his brow onto pages recounting the adventures of heroes on quest. I am reminded of my own long journey, the miles hard fought, and think to tell him I've found that the path to heaven is measured by desire, and not by miles. Instead, I say that when I was a boy, I, too, would read by flashlight late at night—under blankets, so no one would know. But that was long ago, before I grew up and became a man who waits in the dark until his children sleep and dream—a man who softly descends the stairs to turn on the study's lights and speak in poems at last of love.

*fin*

## ABOUT THE AUTHOR

Richard Jones is the author of several books of poetry, including *Country of Air, The Blessing,* and *Apropos of Nothing.* He is also the editor of *Poetry East* and its many anthologies, such as *The Last Believer in Words* and *Bliss.* A professor of English at DePaul University, he lives north of Chicago with his wife and three children.

The Chinese character for poetry is made up of two parts: "word" and "temple." It also serves as pressmark for Copper Canyon Press.

Since 1972, Copper Canyon Press has fostered the work of emerging, established, and world-renowned poets for an expanding audience. The Press thrives with the generous patronage of readers, writers, booksellers, librarians, teachers, students, and funders—everyone who shares the belief that poetry is vital to language and living.

Major funding has been provided by:
Amazon.com
Anonymous
Beroz Ferrell & The Point, LLC
Golden Lasso
Lannan Foundation
National Endowment for the Arts
Cynthia Lovelace Sears and Frank Buxton
Washington State Arts Commission

*For information and catalogs:*
COPPER CANYON PRESS
Post Office Box 271
Port Townsend, Washington 98368
360-385-4925
www.coppercanyonpress.org

The poems have been typeset in Centaur, an old-style serif typeface originally drawn as titling capitals by Bruce Rogers in 1912–14 for the Metropolitan Museum of Art. Headings are set in Bank Gothic, a rectilinear geometric sans serif typeface designed by Morris Fuller Benton for American Type Founders (ATF) in 1930. Book design and composition by Phil Kovacevich. Printed on archival-quality paper at McNaughton & Gunn, Inc.